Life in the Time of

George Washington and the Revolutionary War

Heinemann Library
Chicago, Illinois

Designed by Kimberly R. Miracle and Betsy Wernert.
Printed in China by South China Printing.

11 10 09 08 07
10 9 8 7 6 5 4 3 2 1

Library of Congress Cataloging-in-Publication Data
Trumbauer, Lisa, 1963-
  George Washington and the Revolutionary War / Lisa Trumbauer.
     p. cm. -- (Life in the time of)
  Includes bibliographical references and index.
  ISBN 978-1-4034-9667-6 (hc) -- ISBN 978-1-4034-9675-1 (pb)
  1. Washington, George, 1732-1799--Juvenile literature. 2. Generals--United States--Biography--Juvenile literature.
  3. United States. Continental Army--Biography--Juvenile literature. 4. United States. Continental Army--Military life--Juvenile literature. 5. United States--History--Revolution, 1775-1783--Campaigns--Juvenile literature.
  6. Presidents--United States--Biography--Juvenile literature. I. Title.
  E312.66.T78 2007
  973.4'1092--dc22
  [B]
                                        2006102473

Acknowledgments
The author and publishers are grateful to the following for permission to reproduce copyright material: **p. 4** Corbis;Francis G. Mayer, **p. 5** Corbis/Francis G. Mayer, **p. 6** Corbis/Joseph Sohm/Visions of America, **p. 8** Corbis/Bettmann, **p. 9** Corbis/The Art Archive, **p. 10** Library of Congress, **p. 11** North Wind Picture Archives/North Wind, **p. 12** The Bridgeman Art Library/Private Collection, **p. 13** Corbis/Bettmann, **p. 14** Getty Images/Photographer's Choice, **p. 15** Corbis/Francis G. Mayer, **p. 16** Corbis/Leif Skoogfors, **p. 17** Corbis/Bettmann, **p. 18** The Art Archive, **p. 19** Library of Congress, **p. 20** Corbis/Bettmann, **p. 21** Corbis/Bettmann, **p. 22** The Granger Collection, New York, **p. 23** Corbis/Bettmann, **p. 24** The Granger Collection, New York, **p. 25** Library of Congress, **p. 26** The Granger Collection, New York, **p. 27** Corbis/Bequest of Mrs. Benjamin Ogle Tayloe; Collection of the Corcoran Gallery of Art.

Map illustration on page 7 by Mapping Specialists, Ltd.

Cover photographs of George Washington and the signing of the Declaration of Independence both reproduced with permission of the Library of Congress.

Every effort has been made to contact copyright holders of any material reproduced in this book. Any omissions will be rectified in subsequent printings if notice is given to the publisher.

Contents

Some words are shown in bold, **like this**. You can find out what they mean by looking in the glossary.

Meet George Washington

George Washington was the first president of the United States. George Washington did not want to be president. Other people thought he would be a great president.

George Washington was president from 1789 to 1797.

George Washington led soldiers
during the Revolutionary War.

The United States had just finished fighting a war.
George Washington had been a **general** in that war.
He had led many soldiers into battle. Many people
thought he would be a good leader for a new country.

The Thirteen Colonies

George Washington grew up in a house like this.

George Washington was born in the **colony** of Virginia in 1732. At that time, the United States was not a country. Some parts were ruled by Great Britain. These parts were called colonies.

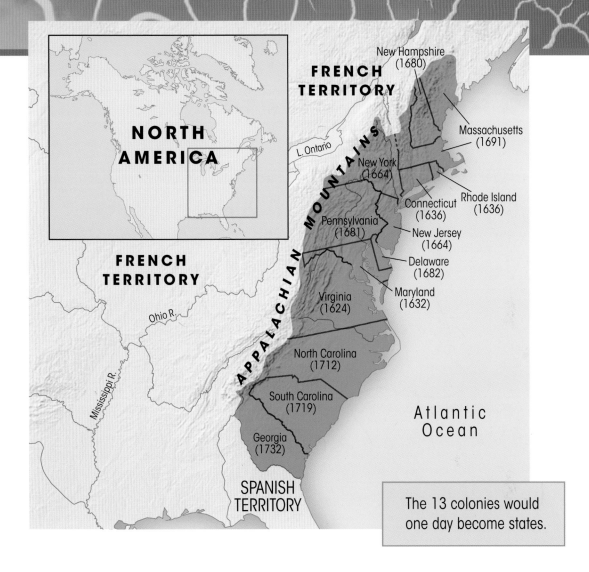

The 13 colonies would one day become states.

Great Britain ruled 13 colonies in all. The colonies were along the east **coast** of **North America**. People who lived in the colonies were called colonists. They had to live by the laws of Great Britain.

Trouble in the Colonies

Some people liked being part of Great Britain, but not everyone liked it. Some people, such as George Washington, were born in the **colonies**. Some people who were born in the colonies felt more American than British.

Colonists did not always agree with British laws—or with each other.

Many colonists did not like Great Britain's king, George III.

People began asking questions about British laws. They wondered why they should listen to a government that was so far away. Many colonists wanted to make and follow their own laws.

The First Shots Are Fired

Many colonists chose not to follow British laws. The king of Great Britain, George III, wanted this to stop. He sent British **troops** to the **colony** of Massachusetts. The colonists did not listen to the British troops.

British soldiers were called "redcoats" because of their red uniforms.

On March 5, 1770, colonists became angry and teased the British troops. The British troops shot at the colonists. This event became known as the Boston **Massacre**. The colonists were very angry.

Five colonists were killed in the Boston Massacre.

The British Are Coming!

The colonists continued to not like or trust the British government. They decided not to pay British taxes or follow British laws. The British government sent more **troops** to the **colonies**.

King George III sent more British troops to the colonies.

Paul Revere's ride happened late at night.

A colonist named Paul Revere rode quickly on horseback to warn the colonists. He shouted that the British were coming. American soldiers met the British soldiers. They fought in the town of Lexington, Massachusetts.

Declaring Independence

The colonists held many meetings in this building in Philadelphia, Pennsylvania.

Many colonists wanted the **colonies** to form their own country. They wanted the colonies to be **united**. They wanted to fight against Great Britain. They did not want to follow British laws anymore.

Not all colonists felt this way. Even so, colonial leaders **declared independence** from Great Britain. A colonist named Thomas Jefferson wrote the Declaration of Independence. The colonies were now the United States of America.

On July 4, 1776, the Declaration of Independence was signed.

The Revolutionary War

Great Britain was not going to let the **colonies** go so easily. The colonists had **declared** their **independence**. By doing so, they had also declared war on Great Britain. They would have to fight for their independence.

The Liberty Bell rang on July 8, 1776, to announce the colonists' declaration.

This war was called the American Revolutio[n] the Revolutionary War. The Battle of Lexingto[n] the war's first battle. Many more battles woul[d] follow. The war would last for many years.

The
was

George Washington's Army

Great Britain had a skilled army. British soldiers had a lot of **training**. The United States did not have a real army. Soldiers were not trained, so they did not know what to do.

The colonial soldiers were called militiamen.

George Washington knew how
to be a good soldier and leader.

The colonial leaders started the Continental Army. They
chose George Washington to be its leader. Washington
had fought in another war. The leaders were certain that
he was the right person for the job.

Victories and Hardships

George Washington and his soldiers had many **victories**. On December 26, 1776, Washington and his soldiers surprised the British army. They beat the British at the Battle of Trenton in New Jersey.

George Washington and his soldiers secretly crossed the Delaware River.

The winter of 1777–1778 was hard for Washington and the Continental Army. The army spent the winter at Valley Forge in Pennsylvania. Their uniforms were old and ripped. They had very little food and supplies.

Many soldiers died during the winter at Valley Forge.

Help from Others

Benjamin Franklin asked the French to help the Americans.

Other countries watched what was happening in the United States. People in France were very interested. France and Great Britain did not always get along. The French decided to help the Americans fight against the British.

Prussia was another country in Europe. An army officer from Prussia **joined** Washington's **troops** at Valley Forge. He **trained** the troops how to be better soldiers and fighters. The training helped.

Friedrich Wilhelm von Steuben trained the soldiers.

The British Give Up

On October 17, 1781, the British **surrendered** to George Washington at the Battle of Yorktown. It was the end of the Revolutionary War. The United States had won its **independence**! It was free from Great Britain.

The British surrendered at the Battle of Yorktown in Virginia.

The Treaty of Paris said all British troops had to leave the United States.

Almost two years passed. Finally, on September 3, 1783, Great Britain and the United States signed the **Treaty** of Paris. The treaty meant that Great Britain **recognized** the United States as a country.

A New Country

The war was over, and the British **troops** were gone. The new country had new problems. It had to set up its government. It also had to decide what laws everyone should follow.

The early leaders were called the Founding Fathers.

George Washington became president on April 30, 1789.

The new country had to decide many things. One decision was not as hard as the rest. They wanted George Washington to be the country's leader. He was **elected** the country's first president in 1789.

If You Grew Up Long Ago

If you grew up in the time of George Washington...

- You would have to walk or ride a horse to get from one place to another.

- You would have to write a letter or visit your family and friends because there were no telephones.

- You would not have factories to make clothing and shoes.

- You would not have televisions to watch what was happening in other places.

- You would not have a microphone so everyone could hear you tell important news.

Timeline

1732   George Washington is born.

1770   The Boston **Massacre** happens.

1775   April 18: Paul Revere makes his famous ride.

       April 19: The first battle of the Revolutionary War is fought in Lexington, Massachusetts.

1776   July 4: The **Declaration** of **Independence** is signed.

       December 25: George Washington and the Continental Army cross the Delaware River.

       December 26: George Washington and the Continental Army beat the British at the Battle of Trenton in New Jersey.

1777–78 Soldiers spend the winter at Valley Forge, Pennsylvania.

1781   The British **surrender** at the Battle of Yorktown in Virginia.

1783   Great Britain and the United States sign the **Treaty** of Paris. The Revolutionary War officially ends.

1789   George Washington is **elected** and becomes the first president of the United States.

1799   George Washington dies.

Find Out More

Books

Ansary, Mir Tamim. *Independence Day*. Chicago: Heinemann Library, 2006.

Burke, Rick. *George Washington*. Chicago: Heinemann Library, 2003.

Ribke, Simone T. *Thomas Jefferson*. New York: Children's Press, 2003.

Weintraub, Aileen. *Read About George Washington*. Berkeley Heights, NJ: Enslow, 2004.

Websites

Library of Congress Kids – Revolutionary War
http://www.americaslibrary.gov/cgi-bin/page.cgi/jb/revolut

National Portrait Gallery – For Kids
http://www.georgewashington.si.edu/kids/portrait.html

White House Kids – Meet the Presidents
http://www.whitehouse.gov/kids/presidents/georgewashington.html

Glossary

coast land next to the ocean

colony place that has been settled by people from another country

declare announce something

elect choose someone by voting

general leader of an army

independence freedom; not belonging to another country or group of people

join come together

massacre killing of many people all at once

North America one of the seven continents on Earth

recognize know who or what someone or something is; understand

surrender give up in a war or battle

train teach someone how to do something

treaty written agreement between two countries or groups

troop group of soldiers

unite join together

victory win in a battle or contest

Index